THE
DREAM
CATCHER

THE
DREAM CATCHER

Unravel the Mysteries of your Sleeping Mind

ELEMENT

Shaftesbury, Dorset ❖ Rockport, Massachusetts ❖ Melbourne, Victoria

© ELEMENT BOOKS LIMITED 1997

Published in Great Britain in 1997 by
ELEMENT BOOKS LIMITED
Shaftesbury, Dorset SP7 8BP

Published in the USA in 1997 by
ELEMENT BOOKS INC.
PO Box 830, Rockport, MA 01966

Published in Australia in 1997 by
ELEMENT BOOKS LIMITED
and distributed by PENGUIN AUSTRALIA LTD.
487 Maroondah Highway, Ringwood, Victoria 3134

Designed by
THE BRIDGEWATER BOOK COMPANY

Picture credits

Bridgeman Art Library pp 2, 20, 31, 45, 67, 105; e.t. archive pp 95, 119

Picture research by

Vanessa Fletcher

Printed and bound in Singapore

British Library Cataloguing in Publication data available

ISBN 1 86204 246 2

day

date

time

day

date

time

day

date

time

day

date

time

day

date

time

day

date

time

day

date

time

day

date

time

day

date

time

day

date

time

day

date

time

day

date

time

day

date

time

day

date

time

day

date

time

day

date

time

dream journal

day _____

date _____

time _____

dream journal

day

date

time

dream journal

day

date

time

day

date

time

day

date

time

day

date

time

day

date

time

day

date

time

day

date

time

day

date

time

day

date

time

day

date

time

day

date

time

day

date

time

day

date

time

day

date

time

day

date

time

day

date

time

day

date

time

day

date

time

day
_____

date
_____

time
_____

day

date

time

day

date

time

day

date

time

day

date

time

day

date

time

day

date

time

day

date

time

day

date

time

day

date

time

dream journal

day

date

time

day

date

time

day

date

time

day

date

time

day

date

time

day _____

date _____

time _____

day

date

time

day

date

time

day

date

time

day

date

time

day

date

time

day

date

time

day _____

date _____

time _____

day

date

time

day

date

time

day

date

time

day

date

time

dream journal

day

date

time

day

date

time

day

date

time

dream journal

day

date

time

day

date

time

day

date

time

day

date

time

day

date

time

day
_____

date
_____

time
_____

day

date

time

day

date

time

day

date

time

day

date

time

dream journal

day

date

time

day

date

time

day

date

time

day

date

time

day

date

time

day

date

time

day

date

time

day

date

time

day

date

time

day

date

time

day

date

time

day

date

time

day

date

time

day

date

time

day

date

time

day

date

time

day

date

time

day

date

time

day

date

time

day

date

time

day

date

time

day

date

time

day

date

time

dream journal

day

date

time

day

date

time

day

date

time

day

date

time

day

date

time

day

date

time

day

date

time

day

date

time

day

date

time

day

date

time

day

date

time

day

date

time

day

date

time

day

date

time

day

date

time

day

date

time

dream journal

day

date

time